WE WERE HERE FIRST
THE NATIVE AMERICANS

THE
SIOUX
OF THE GREAT NORTHERN PLAINS

Pete
DiPrimio

PURPLE TOAD
PUBLISHING

P.O. Box 631
Kennett Square, Pennsylvania 19348
www.purpletoadpublishing.com

WE WERE HERE FIRST
THE NATIVE AMERICANS

The Apache of the Southwest
The Inuit of the Arctic
The Iroquois of the Northeast
The Nez Perce of the Pacific Northwest
The Sioux of the Great Northern Plains

Printing 1 2 3 4 5 6 7 8 9

Publisher's Cataloging-in-Publication Data
DiPrimio, Pete
   The Sioux of the Great Northern Plains / Pete
DiPrimio
      p. cm.—(We were here first. The Native
Americans)
   Includes bibliographic references and index.
         ISBN: 978-1-62469-075-4 (library bound)
         1. Dakota Indians—Juvenile literature. 2.
Indians of North America—Biography—Juvenile
literature. 3. Sioux Nation.   I. Title.
                                          E99.D1 2013
                              978.0049752—dc23
                                          2013946332

eBook ISBN: 9781624690761

Printed by Lake Book Manufacturing, Chicago, IL

CONTENTS

Sitting Bull was a brave warrior and a great leader against an unbeatable U.S. government. He wanted his people to be free and treated with respect. He spent his life trying to make that happen.

CHAPTER 1
VISION OF VICTORY

Sitting Bull was ready to see with closed eyes. He had smoked the medicine pipe, and let the magic do its work. He had danced in the Sun Dance Ceremony, hour after hour, going long after others had collapsed. He had danced until every fiber in his body ached and his mind begged him to stop, despite a bad foot from a 20-year-old war injury.

He could not stop. The vision was coming.

Sitting Bull had danced for 36 straight hours[1] until even his strong legs buckled. Now he sat in front of a small teepee just beyond the Sioux village near the Little Bighorn River. He was a powerfully built man with long, black hair parted in the middle. His bronzed face was deeply lined, as if a sculptor had etched them in. His dark eyes never seemed to blink, making it seem like he could read a person's mind with just a look.

A hot summer sun blazed from a cloudless blue sky in what the white man called the Montana Territory. Sitting Bull had no use for the white man nor his words. War had come again and Sitting Bull wanted to know what was in store for the Sioux.

The dance had left him exhausted and hurting. The pipe's smoke from the pipe had made him dizzy. He welcomed it all.

The vision was coming.

Sitting Bull was a great warrior, but more than that, he was a great chief—a leader, a holy man, one who was loved by the Sioux and feared by the whites.[2] His reputation was so good, his "strong medicine" so well known, that thousands of Native Americans from all across the Great Plains had come to join him. Native Americans had once been free to live in the Great Plains and honor the Great Spirit by living with nature, not destroying it.

Sitting Bull had fought and struggled and, now, danced.

It was all good.

The vision was here.

He saw a great prairie of grass strewn with bodies. They were white soldiers—the Native Americans called them "Blue Coats"—killed in battle.[3] Mighty Sioux warriors walked past them, holding rifles and bows and arrows, and thrusting spears into the air.

Sitting Bull's eyes snapped open.

Victory was coming.

He stood and warriors rushed towards him. A gust blew hard and rattled the brown Dream Catcher hanging from the top of the teepee.

Sitting Bull believed the wind-blown Dream Catcher was a sign from the Great Spirit. He told the warriors what he had seen and what it meant.

"The Great Spirit has given our enemies to us," he said. "We are to destroy them."

One warrior, older, with graying hair, shook his head.

"The white men are too many and too strong. They have brought a famous general, this Custer, to hunt us down like dogs."

Dream Catchers

The Dream Catcher is a small round net with feathers attached. Native Americans believe the air is filled with good and bad dreams. Good dreams pass through the Dream Catcher's center hole to a sleeping person. Bad dreams are caught in the net and are destroyed by the rising sun.

"I know of this Long Yellow Hair," Sitting Bull said, using the name the Sioux often called George Armstrong Custer.[4] "He is reckless. He makes mistakes."

The older warrior wouldn't back down.

"They promise that if we lay down our weapons and move to the reservation, we will have food and medicine and peace."

Sitting Bull glared at him. "They lie."

It was June of 1876. Sitting Bull was 45 years old, young enough to believe in the strength of the Sioux nation, old enough to understand the white man's threat, and brave enough to risk death to save his people.[5]

For a big part of the 19th century the Sioux had ruled the Great Plains that covers what is now North Dakota, South Dakota, Wyoming, and Montana. But by 1850, white settlers had begun moving in, taking land, and spreading violence and disease.[6]

The Sioux needed someone strong to stand up to them, someone like Sitting Bull.

General George Armstrong Custer

He had killed his first buffalo when he was 10, joined his first war party when he was 14. He did so well that his name was changed from Jumping Badger to Sitting Bull (*Tatanka Iyotaka*). He fought the white man for the first time when he was 32. By the time he was 37, he had become chief of the Lakota nation, one of the Sioux's seven tribes.[7]

Sitting Bull would have five wives and four children.[8] He would win battles and lose wars. He would flee to Canada and return home to be imprisoned. He would later join Buffalo Bill's Wild West Show where he would make lots of money and become world-famous.

But he would never compromise, especially when the U. S. government broke treaty after treaty to take more and more land. Millions of buffalo had been slaughtered; thousands of innocent Native Americans had been killed. Sitting Bull believed that a government that did that could not be trusted.[9]

Besides, reservation life wasn't for him; it wasn't for any Sioux.

"So what will you have us do?" the older warrior asked.

Sitting Bull squinted toward the distant horizon. In his mind, he heard war drums beating.

"Let us put our minds together," he said, "and see what life we can make for our children."[10]

The Sioux needed buffalo to survive. The white men did not and slaughtered the animals by the millions. In this 1870 photo, a man stands atop a huge pile of buffalo skulls.

The Legend of Bear Rock or Devil's Tower

Devil's Tower

In Wyoming, there is a great rock formation that rises out of the plains. It is called the Devil's Tower, a white man's name because the Sioux do not believe in the devil. Many Sioux call the tower Bear Rock because its steep sides are streaked and gashed as if attacked by giant bear claws.

A long time ago two young Sioux boys got lost in the prairie. They wandered throughout the land for three days, wishing that someone would find them. But nobody did.

On the fourth day, a huge bear approached them. It was Mato, the giant grizzly. He was hungry and saw the boys as a snack. The boys ran, but Mato ran faster and got closer. The boys began praying to Wakan Tanka, the Creator.

"Tunkashila, Grandfather, have pity, save us," the boys cried to their Creator.

Suddenly, the ground shook and the rock rose beneath them causing a great tower to lift them over a thousand feet into the sky. Mato tried to race after them. He clawed at the rock trying to get them, but couldn't. Finally, he gave up.

The boys were trapped on top of the rock tower until Wanblee, the Great Eagle, took brought them safely back to their village. The boys told their friends and family what had happened. That's why the Sioux call it Bear Rock.[11]

Crazy Horse, once so quiet as a boy he was known as "The Strange One," became a great warrior who fought so his Lakota people could return to their way of life. He helped win the Battle of the Little Bighorn, but not the overall war.

CHAPTER 2
BATTLE OF THE
LITTLE BIGHORN

Crazy Horse was ready for war. He always was. But this time, he hoped, it would drive away the Blue Coats for good.

"I have a good feeling about this," he said to Sitting Bull as the two great chiefs sat on horses overlooking the Little Bighorn River in what is now Montana. It was late June 1876. Somewhere beyond the horizon, U. S. troops were marching towards them. It is time, Crazy Horse thought, to end this.

"You always do," Sitting Bull said. "You never change."

"Maybe, but the face staring back at me when I look in a stream has changed," he said with a sad smile.

"Growing old is part of life," Sitting Bull said.

"That's something I'll never know," Crazy Horse said.

Sitting Bull was silent.

Crazy Horse wasn't crazy, as his name implies, but he was different. His fair skin and brown, curly hair made him stand out from the others. He never wanted his photo taken because he believed a camera would take away his spirit. Because of that, there's only one known photograph of him. Even though he could write, he refused to sign his name to anything, especially a document that might take away the rights of his people. Maybe the "crazy" part of his name really meant "crazy like a fox" because he was shrewd and cunning more than anything else.[1]

Crazy Horse was born with the name *Tashunka Witco,* but according to one report, he changed it when he became a warrior because of the dreams of wild horses he often had.[2]

He first saw danger from the white man in 1854 during the Grattan Massacre. A group of soldiers, led by Lieutenant John Grattan, entered a Sioux camp to arrest the men who had killed a settler's cow. The chief, Conquering Bear, refused to release the men, and violence broke out. The chief was killed and the warriors responded by killing Grattan and 19 of his men.[3]

From that point on, Crazy Horse didn't trust whites. He led a series of attacks against white soldiers, gaining fame with his ability to avoid injury and death on the battlefield. His main goal was to return the Lakota people to their way of life before the whites arrived.[4]

For a little while, that seemed to come true. After a series of wars, the U. S. government signed a treaty in 1868 with the Sioux that promised that the Black Hills in South Dakota, which were sacred to the Sioux people, would be theirs forever.[5]

"Forever" lasted until 1874, when George A. Custer—who was then a lieutenant colonel in the army—found gold in the Black Hills. Within a year, thousands of miners and gold prospectors had swarmed into the area. The U. S. government tried to get the Sioux to sell their land.[6]

But they were not interested in the slightest.

"One does not sell the earth upon which the people walk," Crazy Horse said.[7]

Sitting Bull picked up a handful of dirt and said, "I do not want to sell any land to the government, not even as much as this!"[8]

Since the Native Americans wouldn't sell, the U. S. government ordered them to get out and move onto reservations.

The war was on.

The Native Americans were led by Crazy Horse, Sitting Bull, Gall, and Two Moons. They gathered in Montana to hunt buffalo and antelope, and plan their strategy. Their number grew to 7,000, with 2,500 warriors.[9]

On June 17, 1876, Crazy Horse led 1,200 warriors to drive back General George Crook and his troops, who were heading to attack Sitting Bull near the Little Bighorn. Perhaps the Blue Coats would give up and leave.[10]

Instead, General George Armstrong Custer showed up.

Custer was famous more as a celebrity than as a great general. He was rather flashy with his long, curly blond hair. He had graduated last in his West Point class of 1861. He had been called the "Boy General" because he briefly got that rank at age 23 during the Civil War. It was also during the Civil War that he became famous for having 12 horses shot out from under him. Some saw that as bravery; others saw it as foolishness.[11]

Custer didn't care what others thought and reveled in everything related to his military career, foolhardy or not. As he once said, "I would be willing, yes, glad, to see a battle every day during my life."[12]

He arrived as part of the Seventh Cavalry. He was in charge of a battalion of 600 men.

On June 25, he was told by scouts that they had found a Native American village larger than they had ever seen. Custer didn't care. He had glory on his mind. He split his soldiers into three groups and went looking for trouble.

He found it.

Sitting Bull stayed near the village to handle any Blue Coat attack. Crazy Horse, Gall, and Two Moons led their warriors into battle.

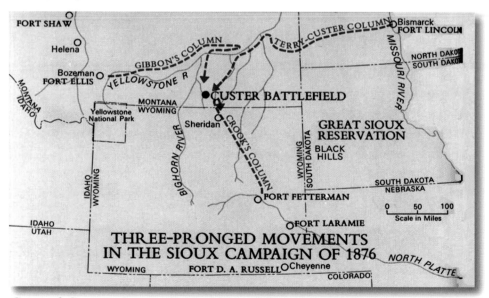

General George Custer divided his soldiers into three groups. It was one of his many mistakes during the Battle of the Little Bighorn.

Around 3:00 p.m. that afternoon, one of Custer's groups—led by Major Marcus Reno—ran into a large Native American force near the Little Bighorn River. After suffering major losses, Reno retreated to a nearby hill. He would not be able to help Custer.

The warriors turned their attention to Custer, who had marched into their village near the river. One of the Sioux leaders, Low Dog, shouted to his men, "This is a good day to die. Follow me."[13]

The Sioux attacked Custer's forces with more than a thousand warriors, rushing down toward them like a human avalanche. Crazy Horse led his men. Two Moons and Gall led theirs.

"It was like a hurricane," a Sioux chief, Kill Eagle, would later say. "It was like bees swarming out of a hive."[14]

Custer ordered his men to fall into a circle. But the Native Americans surrounded them with at least eight times the number of soldiers.

The victory was total. There were no prisoners.

In all, 265 soldiers were killed, and 55 were wounded.[15]

The only survivor on the U. S. side was Comanche, a horse. He lived another 15 years and, to honor him, U. S. Army officials ordered that he never be ridden again.

After Custer's defeat, the U. S. Army went after the Sioux looking for vengeance. Sitting Bull and his followers escaped into Canada. Crazy Horse kept up the attack.

But in the winter of 1877, with food running out and U. S. soldiers pushing hard, Crazy Horse's warriors began leaving him. In May 1877, he rode into Nebraska's Fort Robinson and surrendered.[16]

Crazy Horse was told to stay on the reservation, but that summer he left to help his sick wife. He was arrested and returned to Fort Robinson. When he found out he was going to jail, he fought with the officers and was bayoneted in the kidneys. His father was with him when he died on September 5, 1877.[17]

A huge memorial of Crazy Horse is being carved out of a Black Hills mountain near Mt. Rushmore. It reflects his image as a great leader trying to preserve his people's way of life, no matter what the cost.[18]

Pipe Dreams

The sacred peace pipe was very important in Sioux society. It helped smokers have visions. Here's a legend of how it started.

Two young warriors were walking one night. They ran into a beautiful woman in a stunning dress.

"What a beautiful girl," one warrior said. "I love her. I will marry her."

"No," said the second warrior. "Leave her alone. She might be holy."

The woman held a pipe. She offered it to the sky, then the earth.

"I know what you have been saying," she said. "One of you is good. The other is bad."

She put the pipe on the ground and turned into a buffalo cow. The cow pawed at the ground, picked up the pipe, and turned into a woman again.

"This is a peace pipe," she said. "From now on all treaties and ceremonies will be done after smoking it. It will make you think about peace. You shall offer it to the Great Mystery and to Mother Earth."

The men ran to their village and told everyone what had happened. The leaders went out to see the woman for themselves. She told them what she had told the young men, then added that when they set free the spirit of someone who dies, they must wear a white buffalo cow skin. Then she gave the pipe to the village's medicine men, turned into a buffalo cow, and ran away to the land of the buffalo.

From that day on, the Sioux used a pipe.[19]

Peace pipes such as this Lakota chanunpa pipe stem (it's missing the pipe bowl) were very important in Sioux culture.

The mighty buffalo helped keep the Sioux nation strong.

CHAPTER 3
SIOUX NATION
RISES

Black Coyote scanned the horizon. Behind scattered groups of warriors, women and children followed. Behind them there were more groups, part of a large band of new arrivals to this unclaimed territory now known as North America. They had pushed through the Great Mountains (now called the Rockies) and arrived on fertile land rich in animals to hunt, berries to gather, rivers and lakes to fish and drink.

Black Coyote stood on a rise of land. All he could see in the distant horizon was waving grass of green and gold. White clouds glided across the sky like giant antelope. A light breeze cooled skin warmed by a hot late-afternoon sun. Near the horizon a dark mass moved as if made of a million parts.

It was a buffalo herd too numerous for anyone to count.

It was good, Black Coyote thought to himself. Very good.

"We should stop here and settle for the night," a voice said behind him. It was Gray Elk, his second in command. He had been with Black Coyote for years. Together they had braved the rough travel, brutal weather, and occasional raids of other Native Americans who learned too late the danger of challenging them.

Black Coyote pointed to a bend in the river perhaps a half mile away below them.

"We'll make camp there," he said.

"And then, where?" Gray Elk asked.

"Where the Great Spirit and the buffalo lead us," Black Coyote said.

The Sioux had no use for roots, you see, even before they were called the Sioux.

They were a people on the move, never settling, rarely resting. They lived in *teepees* (also tipis), made of buffalo hide, that were quickly built, quickly torn down, that fit in with their mobile lifestyle. An entire village could be packed up and ready to move in an hour.[1]

Many historians believe that the Sioux were part of a migration of people who traveled from Central Asia across a land bridge on the frozen Bering Sea to North America. It's believed that the migration started some 30,000 years ago. Once they crossed over into the region now known as Alaska, they spread out across what is now Canada and the United States, even down through Mexico and Central and South America.[2]

Black Coyote's people settled in the northern plains, first in what is now Minnesota, then later in North and South Dakota, Wyoming, and Montana.[3]

They called themselves Lakota or Dakota, which means "friends, allies, or to be friendly."[4] Other Native Americans didn't find them so friendly. Some experts say the Chippewa named them Nadowessioux, which means "snake" or "enemy." Others say the Algonquians called them Nadowe Su, which means "little rattle," and refers to a rattle snake.[5] Either way, that name was eventually shortened to the one they are most recognized by: Sioux.

Map Legend:

Lakota Nation: Reserved by the 1868 Treaty for the unreserved use of the Lakota people

Lakota reservations after 100 years of court actions

1876: Lakota reservation after the US stole the Black Hills

Map showing the lands of the Lakota

Horses and teepees were very important in Lakota culture. This photo was taken in 1891.

The Sioux were a proud people who were both fit and fast, which were necessities with the speed and endurance of the animals they hunted. They are believed to be among the first Native Americans to take advantage of the horses that were introduced to America by the Spanish in the late 1500s.

Eventually the Sioux broke into several tribes that were loosely connected in a confederacy. They spoke three different styles of speech, called dialects—Lakota, Dakota, and Nakota.

The Lakota, also called the Teton Sioux (Teton meant prairie dweller), was the largest group. They lived in North Dakota and South Dakota. The Dakota, also called the Santee Sioux, lived in Minnesota and Nebraska. The Nakota lived in North Dakota, South Dakota, and Montana.[6]

By the mid-1800s, there were about 20,000 Lakota. Today, there are around 70,000 with about 20,000 that speak the language.[7]

The Lakota were happy living in Minnesota, hunting deer, elk, and small game, and gathering wild rice and corn. That changed when Europeans, mostly French and British, moved into the area. That pushed other Native Americans into Lakota territory. One group, the Ojibwa, eventually forced the Lakota to move into Wyoming, Iowa, and North and South Dakota, and even Canada. The Lakota adjusted, and began thriving in the 1700s once they got plenty of horses. They became nomads, following the seasonal migration of the buffalo herds.[8]

Other Native American tribes didn't want to interfere with them. But white settlers did as they pushed into Sioux territory. Violence erupted, and government troops got involved. Treaties were made by both and then broken by the whites.

In 1851, the U.S. government called a meeting with all the Native Americans on the Great Plains. If they agreed not to attack white settlers and live in certain areas, the government would give them $50,000 worth of goods per year for 50 years.

That lasted three years.

Violence flared in 1854 near Fort Laramie, Wyoming, when 19 U. S. soldiers were killed in a clash with the Sioux. The next year, U. S. soldiers retaliated by killing about 100 Sioux at their camp in Nebraska. A powerful Indian chief, Red Cloud, launched a war in 1866 that ended in a treaty with the United States giving the Black Hills to the Sioux. Then gold was discovered in the Black Hills and the treaty was broken. In the early 1870s, gold prospectors and miners poured into the area, igniting even more tension.[9]

And then things turned really ugly.

The Sioux were fierce warriors and expert horsemen. They formed war parties to fight those who threatened them, whether it was the U. S. Army or other Native American tribes.

Lakota Creation Myth

The Sioux believe they may be descended from the eagle

A long time ago, when the world was new, the great water monster Unktehi caused a great flood that swept over all the people, smashing them into rocks. Their blood turned into red pipestone, which the Sioux use for their pipes. The red bowl is the flesh and blood of their ancestors; the stem is their backbone; and the rising smoke from the pipe is their breath.

However, one girl survived the flood. A great spotted eagle, called Wanblee Galeshka, swooped down and pulled her from the killer waves. He took her to his home, which was on top of a tall tree on top of the highest peak in the Black Hills. It was the only place not under water.

Some believe Wanblee's home was not in the Black Hills, but rather at the place that is now called Devil's Tower in Wyoming. Both places were sacred to the Sioux.

The eagle took care of the girl, and eventually they fell in love and married. They had twins, a boy and a girl. Eventually the water subsided and the land dried and was rich and fertile. Wanblee carried his wife and children to Earth, telling them to "Be a nation, become a Great Nation—the Lakota Oyate."

The boy grew up to become the only man on Earth. The girl grew up to become the only woman. They had children and the Sioux nation was born.

That is why the Sioux believe they are descended from the eagle, which is considered the wisest of birds and the Great Spirit's messenger. It is why the Sioux wore the eagle plume so proudly, and still do, as a symbol of a great nation.[10]

Great chiefs, such as Little Coyote (also known as Little Wolf) and Morning Star (also known as Dull Knife), thrived in the northern plains.

CHAPTER 4
A FAMILY'S LIFE

Little Wolf was bored. He was stuck in the teepee for the second straight day. Rain pounded the buffalo hide so hard that he wondered if the teepee would collapse. Puddles covered the matted-down grass outside. Still, he was tempted to sneak out and pretend to hunt for buffalo although his mother had been clear about staying inside.

His mother, Radiant Day, was always telling him what to do and at 10 years old he was tired of it. He was big for his age, and fast and strong like no other boy in the camp. Tomorrow he would go on his first buffalo hunt, and he was so excited he could hardly sleep.

His father, Black Tomahawk, had told him to practice with his bow and arrows every day. Little Wolf would have to be very accurate if he was to take down an animal that was over five feet tall weighing almost 2,000 pounds.

During the hunt, Little Wolf would ride a horse and use a spear. He would be with a group of warriors, their faces and arms brightly painted in the Sioux way, often with animal designs.[1] Little Wolf hoped his face would be painted to match that of his father. They'd approach a herd of buffalo, pick one out and begin yelling to get it to run and separate from the herd. Little Wolf

The Sioux used spears and bows and arrows to hunt buffalo. It took a brave and skilled warrior to bring down such a powerful animal.

would try to wound it with the bow and arrow, then finish it off with his spear.

"How old were you when you killed your first buffalo?" he asked his father.

Black Tomahawk was one of the best warriors in the camp. He had a feathered war bonnet, which he only wore during special ceremonies or when going to war. He wore leggings and moccasins, but like all warriors, he rarely wore a shirt. When it got cold, he wore buffalo fur over his shoulders. This was called a buffalo robe.[2]

"I was 10, just like you, but I wasn't as brave," Black Tomahawk said.

Little Wolf closed his eyes and imagined what the hunt would be like, out on the vast prairie, racing the wind on the pony that his father had gotten for him. Sometimes the men would make fires and trick the buffalo into running into traps or over cliffs. Other times they'd use snares to trap them.[3] Little Wolf knew how brave he had to be to hunt such a powerful beast.

His mother's voice broke the moment. "Little Wolf, play with your brother!"

Little Wolf brushed his long, dark hair out of his eyes, and begrudgingly grabbed a top. It was a toy carved from buffalo bone, curved at one end, and pointy at the other. He tossed it at his little brother. Young Elk was only four years old and was always crying and whining. The top wasn't helping, so Little Wolf brought out the bowling balls, which were small stones you could roll. That made Young Elk smile.

Radiant Day wore a long, brown deerskin dress decorated with rabbit fur. She had a couple of such dresses, plus a couple of elk-skin dresses. Her dark hair was long and braided. Everybody had long hair. You only cut it when you were mourning those who had died.[4]

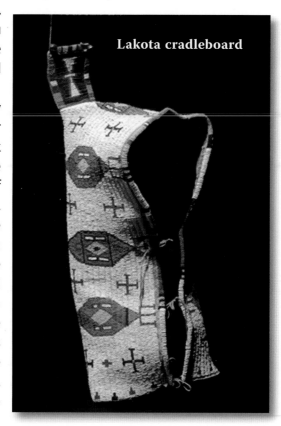

Lakota cradleboard

Radiant Day worked very hard. Unlike many other families, she was Black Tomahawk's only wife, so she had to take care of Little Wolf and his brother all by herself. When they were babies she had carried them on a cradleboard on her back. She cooked, gathered food and firewood, and made deerskin clothes and baskets. She worked with porcupine quills and beads to decorate the clothes and to make star quilts. She also made buffalo pemmican (jerky), an important food because it could be stored for as long as a couple of years.[5]

Radiant Day had told Little Wolf the story of how she and Black Tomahawk were married. They had noticed each other, but Sioux custom didn't allow Radiant Day to talk to him. She couldn't even look at him.[6]

One day, Black Tomahawk showed up near her family's teepee and began playing a love song on a flute. If Radiant Day went outside to listen, it would mean she was interested in marrying him.

The next day she stood outside her teepee, wrapped in a blanket, with her parents beside her. Black Tomahawk came by. She opened her blanket and Black Tomahawk stepped inside the teepee.

That meant that she wanted to marry him, and he wanted to marry her. It also meant Black Tomahawk would have to give Radiant Day's family gifts, usually horses. If the family didn't like the gifts, or if there weren't enough of them, he would be turned away and be disgraced.[7]

Black Tomahawk brought four horses. Radiant Day's father wanted more. Black Tomahawk brought five more horses. The father wanted more. Black Tomahawk brought five more. Her father was about to turn that down, too, but Radiant Day begged him and, finally, he said yes.

So they were married in a big feast that included lots of dancing by the women and then a march through the village.

Radiant Day always smiled when she talked about it. Little Wolf liked it when she smiled.

His stomach rumbled. Fortunately, there was plenty to eat—buffalo, elk, deer, rabbit, and coyote that the men had hunted and fruit, potatoes, and chokecherries that the women had gathered.[8] They had also harvested their own crops. The most important were called the Three Sisters—maize, squash, and beans. They also grew pumpkins. In addition, food was often traded between the tribes.[9]

The Sioux never wasted what they killed—they used all parts of animals for food, clothing, bags, medicines, and other things. If they couldn't find a better use for something, they used it for decoration.[10]

Family was very important to the Sioux. Children were called *wakanisha*, which meant "sacred." While most men had just one wife, they were allowed many if they could afford them.

Men and women had specific roles. The women took care of children and the home, while the men were expected to provide food and other necessities and also to defend the family and the tribe.[11]

War was an important part of Sioux life. Battles showed a warrior's bravery and skill. The more successful a warrior was, the greater the glory he received. That glory was shared by his family.[12]

The Sioux were very religious. They believed in one all-powerful god, called *Wakan Tanka,* or The Great Mystery. The Sioux believed in visions and dreams. They used music and dance to communicate with the spirit world.[13]

The Sioux believed in life after death. They often put a dying person's bed outside to make it easier for the person to ascend to the sky. They were very sad after a death. They would cry until they couldn't talk anymore. Sioux women often cut their hair and ripped off jewelry from their clothes. Men put black paint on their faces.[14]

The Sioux honored their dead. They sometimes used a funeral scaffold for chiefs and warriors to make it easier for the dead person's soul to rise into Heaven.

Only the bravest warriors could wear grizzly bear claw necklaces. They had to do something brave to earn the right to wear them.

The Sioux, both men and women, wore jewelry made out of sea shells, beads, and metal. Men wore necklaces and arm bands. The best necklace a man could wear was one made of grizzly bear claws, but he could only wear one if he did something brave. Women wore bracelets and earrings.[15]

There were lots of rivers and lakes in Sioux territory, and they were crossed in canoes made with frames of willow and sides of buffalo hide.

Mostly, the Sioux traveled over land. Because they did not have wheels, they carried their supplies on a *travois,* which was a sled made of buffalo hide. In fact, the travois often served as their teepee as well. At one time, the Sioux used dogs to pull the travois. Sometimes they'd put supplies in their boats and drag them along.

All that changed once horses became plentiful. It wasn't long before the Sioux were great horse riders who traveled long distances across the Great Plains searching for food and trading with other Native Americans in the region. If tribes didn't understand each other, they could communicate with sign language, which was a universal way for all the Native Americans of the Great Plains to talk to each other.[16]

Religion

The Sioux believed the universe was created by Wakan Tanka, the Great Spirit. Some said Wakan Tanka had a male side, called Tunkashila, and a female side, which was Earth.

There were good and evil spirits.

Sacred pipes were used in ceremonies because the Sioux believed breathing in the smoke put holiness into a person and blowing it out sent a request to Wakan Tanka. Smokers offered the

Statue called "Appeal to the Great Spirit"

pipe to all four directions (north, south, east, and west) to please all the spirits.

The Sioux treated animals as sacred. The most important was the buffalo. The eagle was also important because it was believed to be the messenger between the Sioux and Wakan Tanka.

They believed that everything had a spirit. Underwater spirits controlled animals and plants. Sky spirits were called Thunderbirds, and were the second most powerful spirits behind the Great Spirit.

Each tribe had one medicine man. He performed all the ceremonies during the year. Each ceremony honored one spirit at a time.[17]

The Sioux had four sacred colors: white, yellow, red, and black. They represented the four elements (air, water, fire, and earth) as well as the four directions (north, south, east, and west), the four seasons (winter, spring, summer, and fall) and the four cycles of life (birth, life, death, and afterlife).

When the U.S. Army moved into Sioux territory in 1866, Chief Red Cloud had enough. He started a war that, for a while, kept the Sioux in control of the sacred Black Hills—but only for a while.

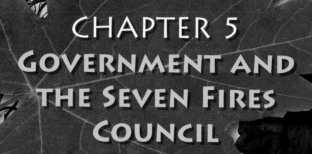

CHAPTER 5
GOVERNMENT AND THE SEVEN FIRES COUNCIL

Black Tomahawk, father of Little Wolf, husband of Radiant Day, sat near the back of a large clearing, near the edge of where firelight kept away the night. The large fire burned brightly, illuminating the dark faces of the somber chiefs who had gathered at this Seven Fires Council to discuss the white-man problem.

Black Tomahawk was a helper for Red Cloud, the powerful chief of the Oglala Lakota tribe. Black Tomahawk could not speak in this meeting. He could watch and think and, later, give Red Cloud his opinion.

The Sioux were like a nation with seven states, except they were called tribes.[1] The Lakota were also divided into tribes.[2] The tribes worked together in trade and war, but this took organization and planning. That meant a government.

For the Sioux, government started with the village council. Each council picked a chief, who served for life. Women were not allowed to be part of the council. The council was divided into smaller groups, with each group having a job to do, like festivals or law and order. The chief would change the jobs each group did every year to make sure no group became more powerful than the other.[3]

Tribes were made up of many villages, with each tribe having a tribal council. Each tribe had a chief. Just like with village councils, the tribal council was divided into smaller groups with specific jobs.[4]

The Seven Fires Council was the main government for the entire Sioux Nation. Each of the seven tribes sent its chief to the council. It made decisions all the tribes followed. It was only for the most powerful chiefs.[5] Sitting Bull was here. So were Crazy Horse and Red Cloud. While the chiefs brought helpers with them, only the chiefs could actually sit at the council and make decisions.

Black Tomahawk was grateful for the opportunity to be with such great chiefs. He was a warrior, as his father had been, and his grandfather, all the way to the beginning. Not every Sioux man had what it took to be a warrior, and that was fine because the Sioux believed in doing what one does best. Some were too gentle or weak or scared. Some had other talents, like being a good hunter or storyteller or a recorder who would paint pictures on buffalo hides that told stories, usually about a great battle or victory. They had entertainers, who told jokes and kept everyone laughing.

Not everyone had what it took to be a member of the Seven Fires Council. Candidates needed qualities found in all great leaders— bravery, kindness, determination, and wisdom.

It was good to laugh, Black Tomahawk thought, but there was no laughter now. The white men were coming.

All the Sioux, men and women, were trained to fight if necessary. Black Tomahawk knew they might need everyone's help in battle. The white men wanted the Sioux's land. They killed the buffalo. They made promises they refused to keep. They took what was not theirs.

It helped that warfare was part of Sioux society. They got into a lot of wars with other tribes, but it was rarely over land. Instead, they fought to prove their courage. They would count coup, which usually meant touching an opponent in battle with a stick without hurting him, or stealing an enemy's horse or weapon, or forcing the tribe to retreat.[6]

They fought with war clubs, bows and arrows, and spears. They used buffalo hide shields for protection and rode into battle on horses.[7]

The Sioux fought with many weapons, including this stone-headed war club. You had to get close to your enemy to use it.

The Sioux were a warrior people.

Battles were always fought away from villages so women and children wouldn't get hurt. Warriors attacked and retreated, always on the move. They almost never fought to the death, and retreated when it was smart to do so, preferring to fight another day.[8]

There would be no retreating with the white men.

"When I was a boy," Sitting Bull said, "the Lakota owned the world. The sun rose and set on their lands. They sent 10,000 horsemen into battle."

"Those days are gone," Red Cloud said. "We no longer have 10,000 horsemen. The white man's diseases have killed off many. Their greedy ways have killed off more."

Black Tomahawk remembered stories of the first fight with the white man, near what was called Fort Laramie, Wyoming. It began in the year the white man called 1854, and it was over some Sioux killing a cow that belonged to a white settler. When white soldiers dared to come into a Sioux camp, they had paid a heavy price. Nineteen of them died.[9]

Many wars were fought in the years that followed, the Sioux giving as good as they got, before a treaty was signed and then broken. So the Seven Fires Council had been called to decide what to do. Black Tomahawk knew that Red Cloud had grown tired of fighting, but the chief would not interfere with the decision of the council.

"If we do not fight," Crazy Horse said, "they will kill us all."

"If we do fight," Red Cloud said, "they will kill us all."

Sitting Bull stood up. Even here, among equals, he was in charge.

"I have lived long enough," he said, repeating a Lakota battle cry. The six other chiefs stood with him. Somewhere in the darkness, war drums began pounding.

Black Tomahawk stood with them.

There would be blood.

Counting Coup

It was very risky for a Sioux to steal a horse. If he were caught, he was usually put to death.

For the Sioux, warfare was like a game where warriors earned points for bravery. The most points were given for touching a live enemy during a battle. More points were awarded for spearing an enemy then shooting him with an arrow.[10]

A warrior also could earn a coup by stealing a horse from another tribe. He would receive more points if he stole a horse that was tied to a teepee than if he stole one in an open field because it was more dangerous.

How dangerous? If someone were caught trying to steal a horse, he was usually killed.

Coups could also be earned by acts of bravery while hunting buffalo and other large animals.

Warriors kept their own count of points. For every coup, a warrior was able to paint his face in a certain way, and wear certain feathers. During a battle, he would wear his war feathers and war paint. This told everybody how great a warrior he was.

Warriors also showed their achievements by painting a picture record of them on the sides of their teepees, or sometimes on the bare sides of their buffalo robes.

Four or more coups allowed a warrior to become a leader in his tribe. Leadership was not passed down from father to son. It had to be earned.[11]

More than a century after the Wounded Knee Massacre, the memory still inspires and moves the Sioux.

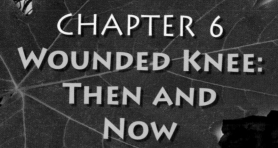

CHAPTER 6
WOUNDED KNEE: THEN AND NOW

Sitting Bull was ready to see with closed eyes. All he wanted to do was dance as he had as a young man, at least for a little while. He was 59 years old, but felt like 100. His body was tired from decades of war; his heart was broken from the white man's lies.

He had asked permission to leave the Standing Rock Indian Reservation in South Dakota and got into trouble. He had followed the rules and it had led to this—a knock at his door at 5:30 a.m. on a cold mid-December morning in 1890.[1]

"You are planning a rebellion," Lieutenant Henry Bull Head said. He was a U. S. Army officer who had been ordered to arrest Sitting Bull.[2]

"No," Sitting Bull said. "I am an old man. The people have asked me to dance. There is no trouble."

Two Native American policemen edged closer to him. They were called Metal Breasts because of their shiny badges. It was not a compliment. Most Lakota believed they had turned on their people for the white man's money.[3]

"This Ghost Dance is stirring up trouble," Lieutenant Bull Head said. "We can't let that happen. We are going to arrest you."

"No," Sitting Bull said quietly. "You are not."

The Ghost Dance was a religious movement, not a rebellion. It was about using songs and chants and a circular dance to convince the Great Spirit to create a new world where there was no white man and the Sioux could live as they had before, in peace and harmony with nature.[4]

Men danced in white cotton or buckskin shirts, brightly painted at the neck and waist, with feathers on the sleeves and symbols everywhere else. Women danced in white cotton robe-like dresses also adorned with symbols and feathers.

The Lakota believed the Ghost Dance costumes kept them safe. The dance was about hope, not war; about faith, not reality. It came from a man called Wovoka, the prophet of peace, who said the white expansion would end peacefully if all Native Americans danced the Ghost Dance. The movement started in Nevada in 1889 and spread swiftly across the West.

In February of 1890, the U. S. government broke yet another treaty with the Lakota, shrinking the size of their South Dakota reservation, forcing them to give up their culture and tradition and take on the white man's ways of farming and raising cattle, and sending their children to boarding schools and teaching them English and Christianity.

But South Dakota was not suitable for farming and the Lakota ran out of food. All the buffalo had been killed years before, and the people were in danger of starving. The Sioux turned to the Ghost Dance to help them get through the tough times.

But this ritual dance scared white settlers and government agents. Troops were called in. The government thought Sitting Bull was about to join the Ghost Dancers and cause big trouble.[5]

Bull Head led Sitting Bull outside and ordered him to mount a horse. Sitting Bull refused and the Metal Breasts tried to force him onto one. A Sioux, Catch-the-Bear, raised a rifle and shot Bull Head, who then fired his revolver into Sitting Bull's chest. A Metal Breast named Red Tomahawk also shot Sitting Bull in the chest and killed him instantly.[6]

A lot of Lakota were angry about his death. More troops were sent in to keep the peace. On December 29, 1890, the Army's Seventh Cavalry—the same group that had been defeated by the Sioux in the Battle of the Little Bighorn—surrounded a group of Ghost Dancers under Lakota chief Big Foot near Wounded Knee Creek. The cavalry demanded that the Ghost Dancers surrender. A fight broke out, a gun was fired and 150 Native

Americans were killed, nearly half were women and children, almost all of them were unarmed.[7]

Was it revenge for the Little Bighorn defeat? No one would ever know.

A Lakota chief, Black Elk, heard the early morning gunshots. He and about 20 warriors raced toward the sound of the shots. They arrived to see bodies everywhere.

"When I saw this," he said, "I wished I had died, too."[8]

Instead, it was a war that died. The battles between the Sioux and the white men were over.

Or were they?

Wounded Knee Revisited

In 1968, the American Indian Movement (AIM) was founded by young Native Americans to publicize the struggles of their people. They wanted to restore pride in their culture and challenge a government that continued to ignore their concerns. AIM sometimes used violent demonstrations and this bothered older Native American leaders.[9]

In 1973, about 200 AIM members and supporters took over the small town of Wounded Knee, the site of the 1890 massacre. This led to a 71-day standoff with federal authorities that included almost nightly gunfire. Hundreds of arrests were made, two Native Americans were killed, and a federal marshal was shot and permanently paralyzed before the standoff ended.[10]

AIM leaders Russell Means and Dennis Banks were put on trial for the violence. The judge finally released them because of evidence that showed that the FBI had manipulated key witnesses.

Means stayed active in Native American causes, and was one of the first to urge U. S. sports teams to stop using Native American names as mascots. He later became an actor. His biggest role was in the 1992 movie, "The Last of the Mohicans." He played the Native American Chingachgook. He died in October of 2012 at age 72 from throat cancer.[11]

The Sioux Today

The Sioux remain a proud people who refuse to sell their heritage. In 1980, the U. S. Supreme Court ruled the Sioux were entitled to about $106 million for the U. S. government's unjust taking of the Black Hills from them in violation of the Treaty of Fort Laramie in 1868. The Sioux have refused to take the money because they don't want to give up their rights to the Black Hills.[12]

Over 100,000 Sioux live in the United States, and more than 10,000 live in Canada. They live mostly in North Dakota, South Dakota, Nebraska, Minnesota, and Saskatchewan in Canada. Many of them live in reservations, areas reserved just for them. In a lot of ways, it's just like a small country, although they are considered citizens of the United States and Canada. They have their own government, laws, police, schools and even a tribal college. They have brought back Sun Dance ceremonies that the U. S. government once banned.[13]

Their political leader is called an *Itancan* in the Lakota and Dakota language, which means "chief" or "president." The Itancan used to be a man chosen by tribal council members. Today, it can be a woman chosen by a vote, just like a mayor or governor.

The Pine Ridge Indian Reservation in South Dakota is the second largest in the United States. Many Native Americans farm and ranch, and raise bison. The Shakopee Mdewakanton Sioux have a large casino on their Minnesota reservation. The Oglala have a casino at Pine Ridge, but because it is one of the poorest areas in the country, the casino often struggles.

Living on a reservation is hard. Native Americans deal with violence, problems associated with alcohol and drugs, and despair. The school dropout rate approaches 62 percent in some places. About 80 percent of the people are often without work, which is 10 times the national average. Native Americans are twice as likely to commit suicide as other Americans.[14]

The Sioux live in modern houses or apartments. They still wear moccasins and beaded vests like their ancestors, but they also wear modern clothes like jeans. They only wear feathers in their hair for special occasions, like ceremonial dances. The women are known for making beautiful quillwork and bead work. Men are famous for their buffalo-hide paintings. Sioux artists also make pottery, *parfleche*, and ceremonial calumets (pipes carved from catlinite).

It is not the life Sitting Bull would have wanted for his people. But as he learned, you don't always get what you want. Sometimes, you have to make the best of what you have.

Sioux Mythology

Thunderbird (also called Wakinyan) was a powerful sky spirit.

The Sioux had many mythological figures.

Iktomi (also spelled Unktomi or Inktomi) was tricky and his name means "spider." He's also been called Spider-man, but not like the comic book superhero. He usually got into trouble, breaking rules and acting silly or stupid. Many of the stories about him are funny. But sometimes they are violent and serious, and used as examples to watch out for danger.

Coyote (Mica or Maca) was like Iktomi because he was a troublemaker. He sometimes turned into a man or sometimes remained a coyote.

Thunderer (Wakinyan) was also known as Thunderbird. He was a powerful sky spirit who soared like a giant bird with wings that made the sound of thunder and eyes that shot out bolts of lightning. In Sioux mythology, he was the enemy of the horned snake Unktehi, a water monster.

Double Face (Hestovatohkeo'o) was a nasty monster who looked like a man except he also had a second face on the back of his head. Double Face would kill anyone who looked his second face in the eye. He constantly tried to persuade his victims to do just that.[15]

41

1. Sitting Bull had five wives: Light Hair, Four Robes, Scarlet Woman, Snow-on-Her, and Seen-by-her-Nation.

2. He had four children: Crow Foot (son), Many Horses (daughter), One Bull (adopted son), Walks Looking (daughter).

3. Crazy Horse's real name was Tashunka Witco. He was born in 1842 and died in 1877.

4. Sitting Bull has a college named for him. On March 6, 1996, Standing Rock College in Fort Yates, North Dakota, changed its name to Sitting Bull College.

5. A Sioux man sometimes tried a love potion made by a medicine man to make the woman he loved fall in love with him. This was powerful medicine and if the man wasn't careful, it would make him very sick.

6. Because Sioux men were expected to prove their bravery, and because they had to be able to give nice wedding presents to their brides' families (sometimes 20 or more horses), they were often a lot older than their wives, sometimes by as many as 20 years.

7. Because there were more women than men due to deaths from wars and hunting, Sioux men could have more than one wife. They often married sisters to keep jealousy and bickering between families at a minimum.

8. Sioux boys could start hunting buffalo when they were ten years old.

9. There are seven major Sioux tribes: Mdewakanton, Sisseton, Teton, Wahpekute, Wahpeton, Yankton, and Yanktonai.

10. The Sioux believed that sweating helped remove evil spirits from the body.

Chapter 1

1. Sitting Bull Biography, http://www.biography. com/people/sitting-bull-9485326

2. Bill Yenne, *Sitting Bull.* (Yardley, PA: Westholme Publishing, 2008), pp. 56–58.

3. Robert M. Utley, *The Lance and the Shield, The Life and Times of Sitting Bull.* (New York: Henry Holt & Co., 1993). p. 28.

4. James Donovan, *A Terrible Glory: Custer and the Little Bighorn.* (New York: Little, Brown & Co., 2008), p. 28.

5. Utley, p. 35.

6. Sioux Indians, http://www.indians.org/articles/ sioux-indians.html

7. Sitting Bull Biography, http://www.biography. com/people/sitting-bull-9485326

8. Ibid.

9. Yenne, p. 21.

10. Utley, p. 111.

11. Legend of Devils Tower, http://www.first people.us/FP-Html-Legends/A-Legend-Of-Devils-Tower-Sioux.html

Chapter 2

1. Crazy Horse Biography, http://www.biography. com/people/crazy-horse-9261082

2. Ibid.

3. Ibid.

4. Ibid.

5. Ibid.

6. Ibid.

7. Donovan, p. 147.

8. Ibid., p. 186.

9. Ibid., p. 267.

10. Ibid., p. 270.

11. Ibid., p. 275.

12. Ibid., p. 276.

13. Ibid., p. 280.

14. Ibid., p. 282.

15. Ibid., p. 283.

16. Ibid.

17. Crazy Horse Biography, http://www.biography. com/people/crazy-horse-9261082

18. Ibid.

19. Ibid.

Chapter 3

1. The Great Sioux Nation, http://www. legendsofamerica.com/na-sioux.html

2. Guy Gibbon, *The Sioux: The Dakota and the Lakota Nation.* (Malden, MA: Blackwell Publishing, 2003), pp. 17–19.

3. Sioux Indians, http://www.indians.org/articles/ sioux-indians.html

4. The Great Sioux Nation, http://www. legendsofamerica.com/na-sioux.html

5. Gibbon, p. 33.

6. The Great Sioux Nation, http://www. legendsofamerica.com/na-sioux.html

7. Sioux Language, http://www/alsintl.com/ resources/languages/Sioux

8. Dwight Zimmerman, *Saga of the Sioux.* (New York: Henry Holt & Co., 2011), p. 25.

9. The Great Sioux Nation, http://www. legendsofamerica.com/na-sioux.html

10. Lakota Creation Myth, http://www. indianlegend.com/lakota/lakota_001.htm

Chapter 4

1. Sioux Indians, http://nativeamericans.mrdonn. org/plains/sioux/siouxnationtribes.html

2. Ibid.

3. Courtship, http://www.aaanativearts.com/ mailbag-archive/1476-cherokee-and-sioux-courtship-and-wedding-customs. html#axzz2BYGun9s3

4. Ibid.

5. Sioux Indians, http://nativeamericans.mrdonn. org/plains/sioux/siouxnationtribes.html

6. Courtship, http://www.aaanativearts.com/ mailbag-archive/1476-cherokee-and-sioux-courtship-and-wedding-customs. html#axzz2BYGun9s3

7. Ibid.

8. Sioux Indians, http://nativeamericans.mrdonn. org/plains/sioux/siouxnationtribes.html

9. Ibid.

10. Ibid.

11. Ibid.

12. Ibid.

13. Ibid.

14. Sioux Indians, http://nativeamericans.mrdonn. org/plains/sioux/siouxnationtribes.html

15. Ibid.

16. Ibid.

17. Ibid.

Chapter 5

1. Sioux Indians, http://nativeamericans.mrdonn. org/plains/sioux/siouxnationtribes.html

2. Ibid.

3. Ibid.

4. Ibid.

5. Ibid.

6. Ibid.

7. Ibid.

8. The Great Sioux Nation, http://www. legendsofamerica.com/na-sioux.html

9. Ibid.

10. Sioux Indians, http://nativeamericans.mrdonn. org/plains/sioux/siouxnationtribes.html

11. Ibid.

Chapter 6

1. James McLaughlin, "An Account of Sitting Bull's Death." http://www.pbs.org/weta/ thewest/resources/archives/eight/sbarrest.htm

2. Ibid.

3. Waldman, p. 47.

4. Massacre at Wounded Knee, http://www.history. com/topics/wounded-knee

5. Sitting Bull Biography, http://www.biography.com/ people/sitting-bull-9485326

6 James McLaughlin, "An Account of Sitting Bull's Death." http://www.pbs.org/weta/thewest/ resources/archives/eight/sbarrest.htm

7. Massacre at Wounded Knee, http://www.history. com/topics/wounded-knee

8. Peter Mattiessen, *In the Spirit of Crazy Horse* (New York: Viking Penguin Group, 1991), p. 58.

9. Massacre at Wounded Knee, http://www.history. com/topics/wounded-knee

10 Ibid.

11. "Russell Means, Indian Activist, actor, dies at 72." http://www.latimes.com/news/obituaries/ la-russell-means-indian-activist-actor-dies- at-72-20121022,0,3901740.story

12. The Great Sioux Nation, http://www. legendsofamerica.com/na-sioux.html

13. Ibid.

14. Ibid.

15. Sioux Legends, http://www.native-languages.org/ sioux-legends.htm

FURTHER READING

Books

Bonvillain, Nancy. *The Teton Sioux.* New York: Chelsea House Publishers, 1994.

Brindell Fradin, Dennis. *Custer's Last Stand.* New York: Marshall Cavendish Benchmark, 2007.

Burgan, Michael. *The Lakota.* New York: Marshall Cavendish, 2009.

Dolan, Terrance. *The Teton Sioux Indians.* Mexico City: Chelsea Juniors, 1995.

Haldane, Suzanne, and Jacqueline Left Hand Bull. *Lakota Hoop Dancer.* New York: Dutton Children's Books, 1999.

Landau, Elaine. *The Wounded Knee Massacre.* New York: Children's Press, 2004.

Waldman, Neil. *Wounded Knee.* New York: Atheneum Books for Young Readers, 2001.

Works Consulted

Brown, Dee. *Bury My Heart at Wounded Knee.* New York: Holt Paperbacks, 2007.

Cox Richardson, Heather. *Wounded Knee.* New York: Basic Books, Perseus Books Group, 2010.

DiSilvestro, Roger L. *In the Shadow of Wounded Knee.* New York: Walker & Co., 2005.

Donovan, James. *A Terrible Glory: Custer and the Little Bighorn.* New York: Little, Brown & Co., 2008.

Gibbon, Guy. *The Sioux: The Dakota and the Lakota Nation.* Malden, MA: Blackwell Publishing, 2003.

Larson, Robert W. *Red Cloud: Warrior-Statesman of the Lakota Sioux.* Norman, OK: University of Oklahoma Press, 1999.

Mattiessen, Peter. *In the Spirit of Crazy Horse.* New York: Viking Penquin Group, 1991.

"Russell Means, Indian Activist, actor, dies at 72." http://www.latimes.com/news/obituaries/la-russell-means-indian-activist-actor-dies-at-72-20121022,0,3901740.story

Utley, Robert M. *The Lance and the Shield, The Life and Times of Sitting Bull.* New York: Henry Holt & Co., 1993.

Viola, Herman J. *Little Bighorn Remembered.* New York: Times Books, 1999.

Yenne, Bill. *Sitting Bull.* Yardley, PA: Westholme Publishing, 2008.

Zimmerman, Dwight. *Saga of the Sioux.* New York: Henry Holt & Co., 2011.

On the Internet

A Legend of Devil's Tower
http://www.firstpeople.us/FP-Html-Legends/A-Legend-Of-Devils-Tower-Sioux.html

Crazy Horse Biography
http://www.biography.com/people/crazy-horse-9261082

Dakota and Lakota Sioux Language
http://www.native-languages.org/dakota.htm

Great Sioux Nation
http://www.legendsofamerica.com/na-sioux.html

Lakota Creation Myth
http://www.indianlegend.com/lakota/lakota_001.htm

Lakota and Dakota Sioux Fact Sheet
http://www.bigorrin.org/sioux_kids.htm

Map of Sioux Indians
http://www.native-languages.org/sdakota.htm

Massacre at Wounded Knee
http://www.history.com/topics/wounded-knee

Pyramid Mesa Ghost Story
http://www.pyramidmesa.com/bsioux9.htm

Red Cloud Biography
http://www.biography.com/people/red-cloud-9453402

Sioux Indians
http://www.indians.org/articles/sioux-indians.html

Sioux Legends
http://www.native-languages.org/sioux-legends.htm

Sioux Nation
http://nativeamericans.mrdonn.org/plains/sioux/siouxnationtribes.html

Sitting Bull Biography
http://www.biography.com/people/sitting-bull-9485326

Star Quilt Picture
http://nativeamericans.mrdonn.org/plains/sioux/starquilts.html

Story of the Peace Pipe
http://www.indianlegend.com/sioux/sioux_005.htm

American Indian Movement (AIM)—An organization created to publicize Native American struggles in the United States.

buffalo—Ox-like animals, also called bison. They roamed the Great Plains of North America by the millions before European settlers arrived.

cavalry—A military force that fights on horseback.

Dakota—A branch of the Sioux Indians.

FBI—Federal Bureau of Investigation; government police organization that fights crime.

ghost dance—A Sioux dance that was believed to help remove evil from the world and help the dancers return to their traditional way of life.

Lakota—A branch of the Sioux Indians.

migration—The movement from one place or country to another.

parfleche—A Native American rawhide bag often used for holding dried meats.

reservation—An area set aside by the U. S. Government for Native Americans to live.

teepee—A type of tent, made of buffalo hide, that Native Americans used as houses on the Great Plains.

MEET THE
AUTHOR

Pete DiPrimio is an award-winning Indiana sports writer and columnist, a veteran children's author, and a long-time freelance writer. He's also a journalism adjunct lecturer and fitness instructor.